Grits fo

by Glenda Loftin

With Illustrations by the Author

Down Home Press, Asheboro, N. C.

Copyright 1994 by Glenda Loftin

All rights reserved. No part of this book may be reproduced by any means without permission of the publisher, except for brief passages in reviews and articles.

ISBN 1-878086-29-4

Library of Congress Catalog Card Number
94-071654

Cover Design by Ginger F. Harris
Cover Illustration by Glenda Loftin
Book Design by Ginger F. Harris

1 2 3 4 5 6 7 8 9 10

Down Home Press
PO Box 4126
Asheboro, N.C. 27204

Foreword

The scary thing about this book is that it isn't all fiction. It's a humorous exaggeration of the escapades of southerners among us who get by in spite of what is perceived by carpetbaggers and other outlanders as a lack of gray matter. I like to think instead that we're sometimes just a little careless with our day-to-day reasoning practices.

For example, I once entered a residence near the Flat Rock Playhouse in the mountains of North Carolina with my husband, our youngest son and his friend in tow, thinking I was in Carl Sandburg's house, a national historic site.

A woman broke away from a cluster of punch drinkers around the piano and approached us with some concern. "Could I help you?"

"No thanks," I replied cheerily, dismissing her with a wave and mounting the carpeted steps before me, "I think we'll just have a look around upstairs."

I was about a third of the way up when I heard her say, "Excuse me," and turned to see that her concern had become alarm.

"This is the Carl Sandburg Home isn't it?" I said.

"No, ma'am, it is not!"

It was on that eternal walk back to our car that my husband coined the phrase, "Grits for Brains."

I heard the term again the day I took him to my sainted Aunt Bertha's wake. We marveled at the number of people who had come to the funeral home to pay their last respects. Many we had never seen before.

There was much hugging and countless stories of Auntie's acts of kindness. I introduced myself as Bryan's oldest child and within 10 minutes we had been invited to a couple of family reunions and an all-night gospel sing.

Soon it was time to say our last good-bye. When my husband and I approached the casket, I looked down into the face of some strange little blue-haired lady I'd never seen before.

"James," I said, just before the absurdity of it all hit me and I began to snort uncontrollably into my handkerchief, "This is definitely not Aunt Bertha."

Aunt Bertha was lying in repose at the town's only other funeral parlor, two blocks down the street.

Sometime later, I thought about the "Grits for Brains" remark and decided that by exaggerating my own experiences and those of family and friends and by concocting blatant lies, I could assemble a cast of characters in situations that would qualify them for Grits for Brains status.

In this book, I'm the Mrs. Geezenslaw who was prepped incorrectly for surgery. (The woman in charge had a straight razor, a bad attitude and not the best job in the world, so no matter what the doctor had told me, I thought it best to accept what the hospital called the Willie Nelson goatee trim and not insist on the full Yul Brynner cut.)

As for making tossed salad from ketchup and mustard, I believe they were indeed considered vegetables, for a time during the Reagan administration.

And I actually did read a headline in one of those supermarket tabloids telling of a man who had done his own hair transplant from the fur in his armpit.

Finally, I did nickname Mama's old muskrat stole "Clyde," because it turned the exact shade of orange as Clint Eastwood's orangutan in the movie *Every Which Way But Loose*, but that's all I'll own up to — OK, I also put the ribbed condoms in Mama's grocery cart and she did throw them at me, but nobody threw a chicken and nobody got arrested.

To my husband, James, our sons, Jim, Scott and Blake,
my brother, Bryan, the rest of my family
and other assorted Tar Heel trash whose inspiration helped
make this book a reality.

Grits for Brains

You Know You or Your Kinfolk Have **Grits for Brains** *When...*

Grandpa starts looking forward to going senile, because he thinks it has something to do with a trip to Egypt.

You Know You or Your Kinfolk Have **Grits for Brains** *When...*

Cousin Dinette loses her part-time job at the hospital because she preps old lady Geezenslaw incorrectly for surgery and the doctor lifts the sheet expecting to see Yul Brynner only to come face to face with Willie Nelson.

You Know You or Your Kinfolk Have **Grits for Brains** *When...*

Aunt Nola says she married Uncle Homer because he was too ugly to kiss goodbye.

You Know You or Your Kinfolk Have **Grits for Brains** *When...*

The last time the TV weathercaster said the word "freeze" everybody in your living room "assumed the position" and waited for the handcuffs.

Somebody tells your mama she has ancestors and she goes to the doctor to find a cure.

Aunt Famica puts the rag-top down on her convertible, gets out, locks the keys inside, and walks three blocks to a phone booth to call for assistance.

You Know You or Your Kinfolk Have **Grits for Brains** *When...*

Your sister-in-law believes ketchup and mustard are vegetables, and doesn't understand why the tossed salad isn't turning out right.

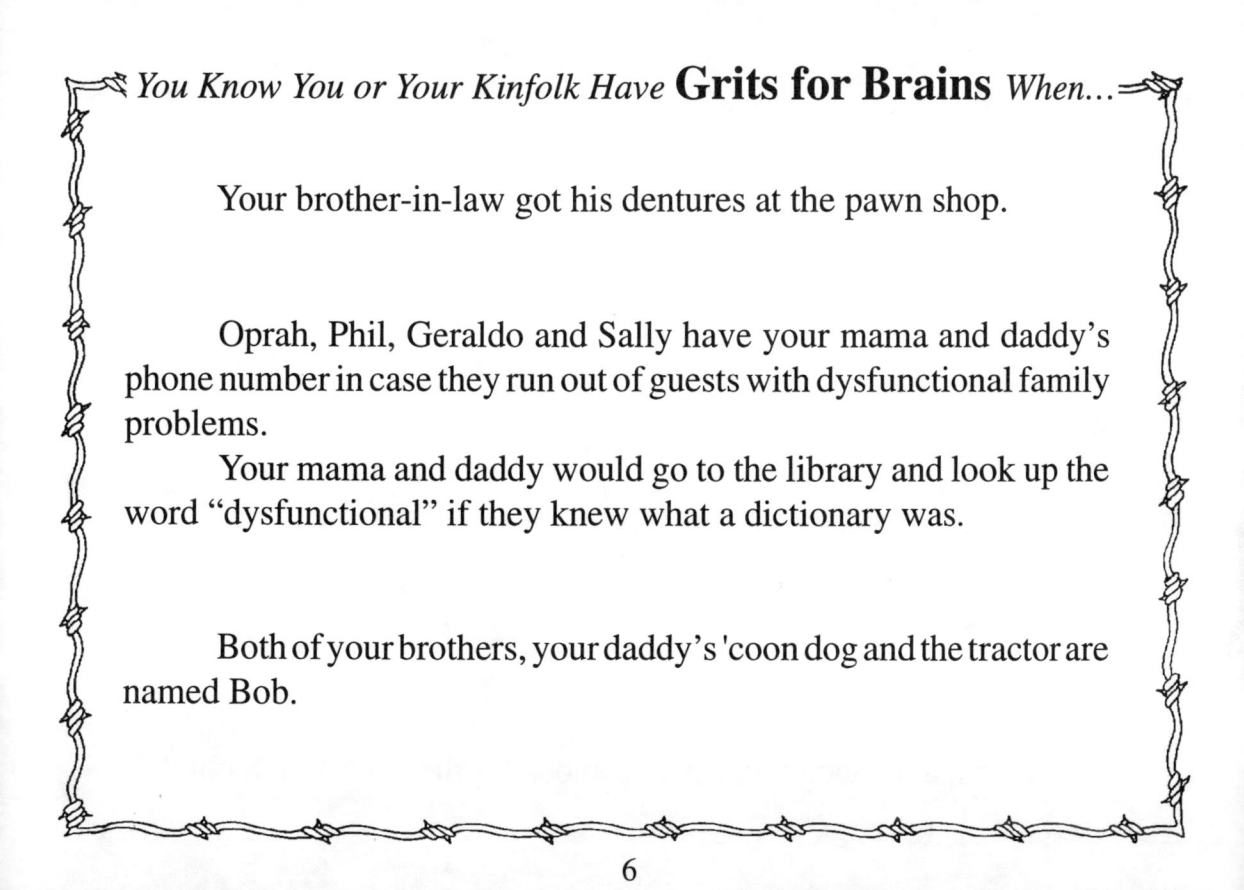

You Know You or Your Kinfolk Have **Grits for Brains** *When...*

Your brother-in-law got his dentures at the pawn shop.

Oprah, Phil, Geraldo and Sally have your mama and daddy's phone number in case they run out of guests with dysfunctional family problems.

Your mama and daddy would go to the library and look up the word "dysfunctional" if they knew what a dictionary was.

Both of your brothers, your daddy's 'coon dog and the tractor are named Bob.

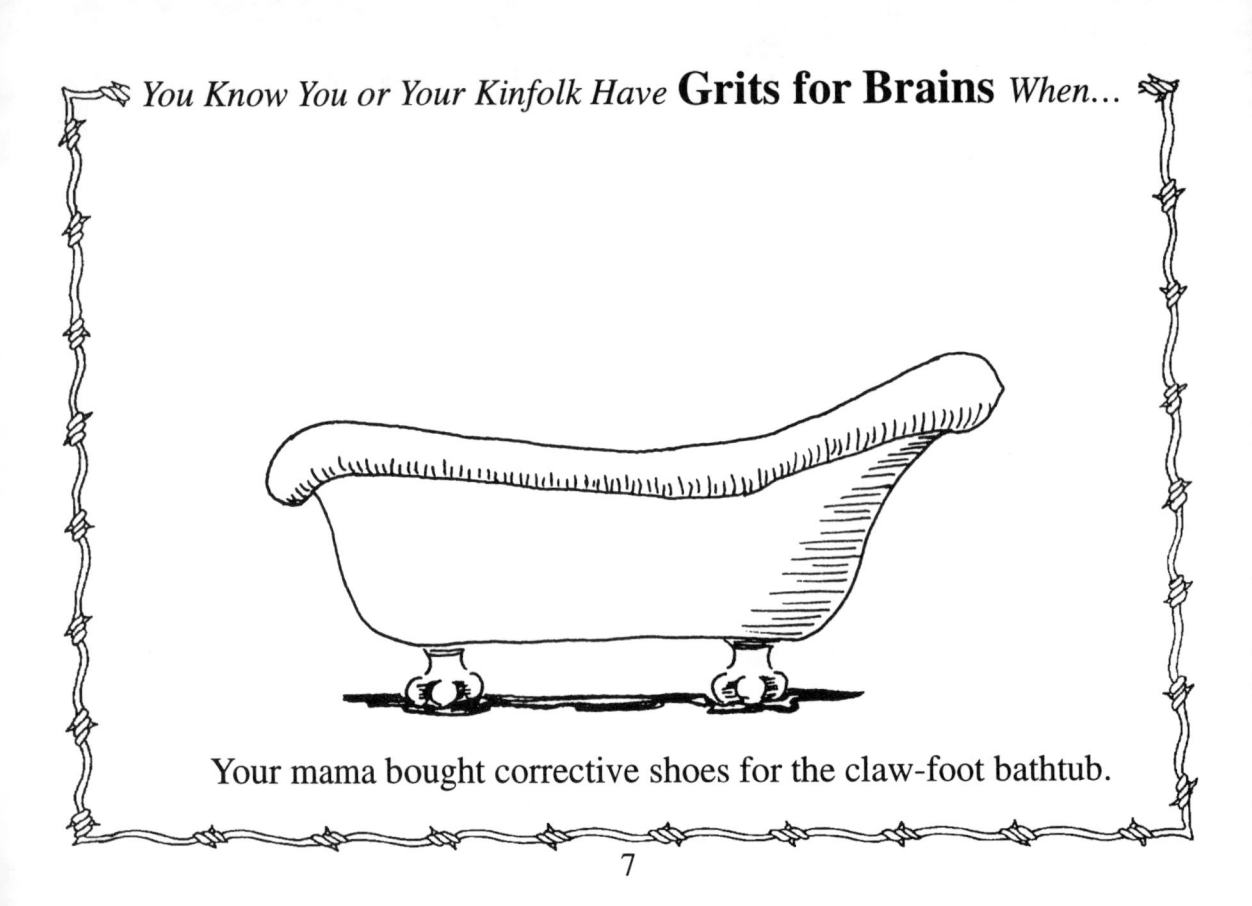

You Know You or Your Kinfolk Have **Grits for Brains** *When...*

Your mama bought corrective shoes for the claw-foot bathtub.

You Know You or Your Kinfolk Have **Grits for Brains** *When...*

Uncle Valise walks into the house and can't decide whether a varmint has died in the wall or his wife has started supper.

You Know You or Your Kinfolk Have **Grits for Brains** *When...*

There's a bumper sticker on your mule that says, "I brake for dead 'possums."

You have a hard time convincing your slow sister Shirley that there's no book of Edna in the Old Testament and Noah was not married to Joan of Ark.

Aunt Vague is planning her spring garden and asks you to bring her a packet of succotash seeds.

You Know You or Your Kinfolk Have **Grits for Brains** *When...*

Your sister can't figure out how shoulder pads work and people keep asking how she got those humps on her back.

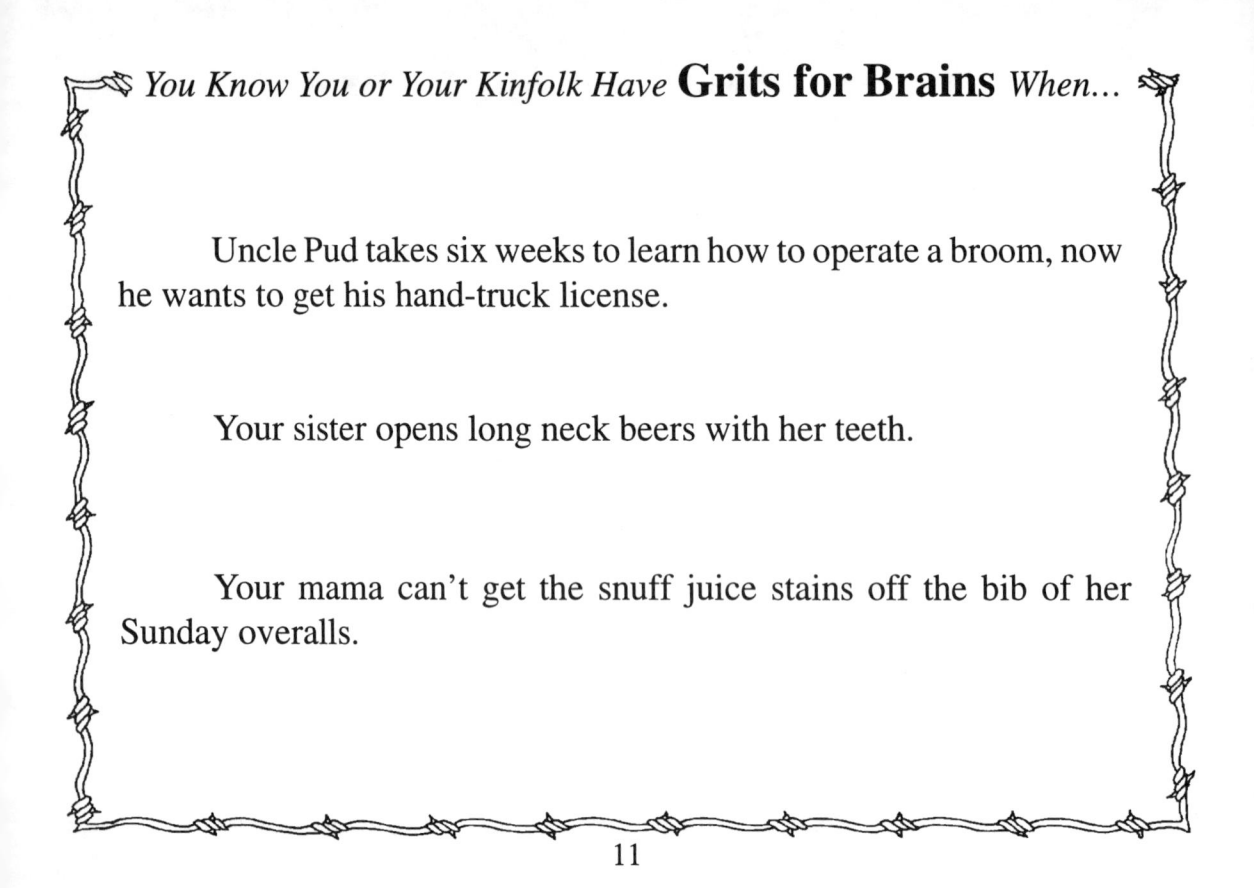

You Know You or Your Kinfolk Have **Grits for Brains** *When...*

Uncle Pud takes six weeks to learn how to operate a broom, now he wants to get his hand-truck license.

Your sister opens long neck beers with her teeth.

Your mama can't get the snuff juice stains off the bib of her Sunday overalls.

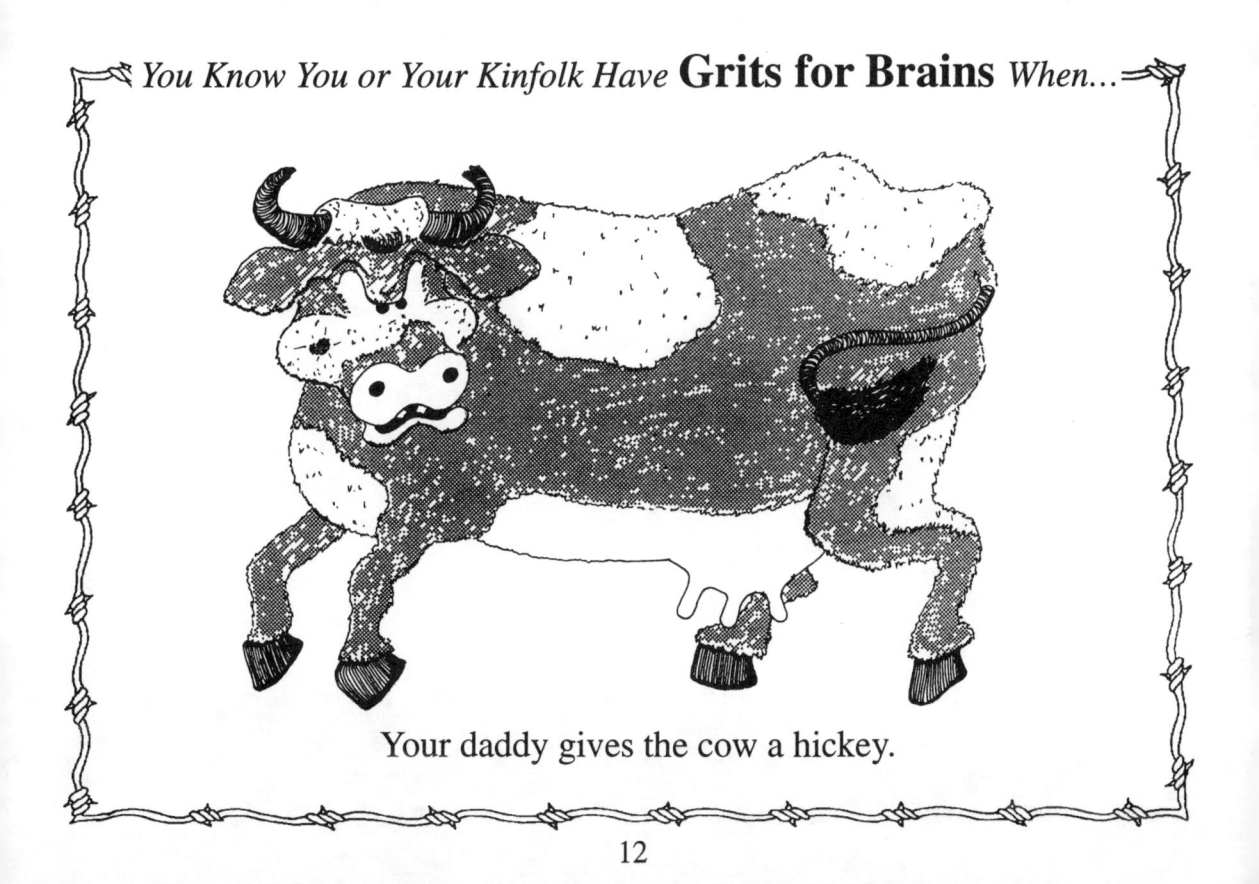

You Know You or Your Kinfolk Have **Grits for Brains** *When...*

Your daddy gives the cow a hickey.

You Know You or Your Kinfolk Have **Grits for Brains** *When...*

Cousin Riley has watched so much TV, he thinks Columbo discovered America, but you know he invented frozen yogurt.

Uncle Slackjaw teaches you that a RCH (red crotch hair) is a unit of measurement. "Cut me another plank son, this un's about one RCH too long."

Cousin Dence bought his mama a microwave oven, but she sent it back because it wouldn't pick up the *Dukes of Hazard*.

You Know You or Your Kinfolk Have **Grits for Brains** *When...*

Instead of fuzzy dice, Cousin Ray hangs his girlfriend's diaphragm from his rear view mirror. Now she has to find another shower cap.

Cousin Delbert charges 50 cents a car for folks to drive by his service station to see a grease stain that has taken on the likeness of Billy Ray Cyrus.

Uncle Mooney claims he has so much static electricity in his body he can light his way to the outhouse just by rubbing his head.

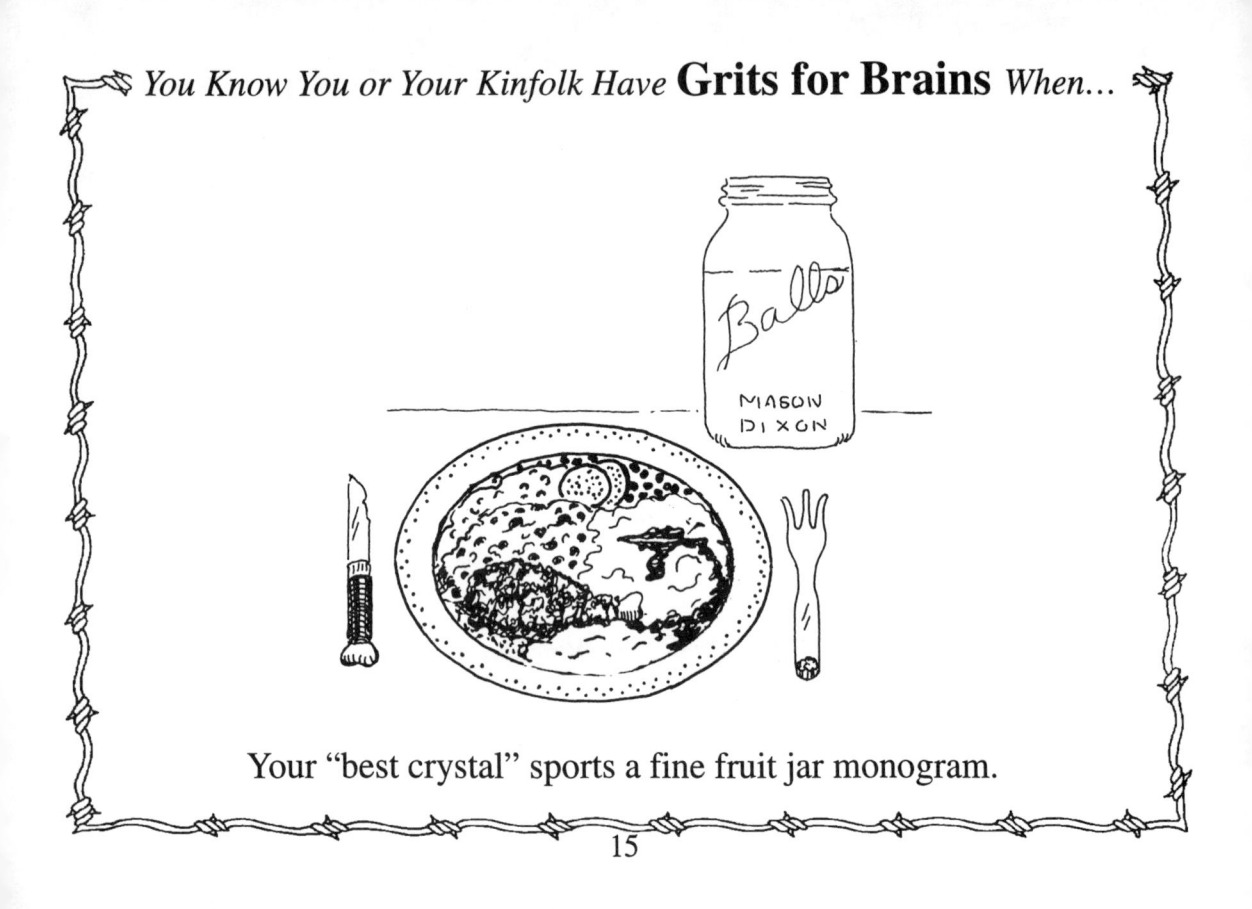

You Know You or Your Kinfolk Have **Grits for Brains** *When...*

Your "best crystal" sports a fine fruit jar monogram.

You Know You or Your Kinfolk Have **Grits for Brains** *When...*

Granny gets homesick and you take her down to the local Chintzy-Mart, hit a few speed bumps, then do a couple of donuts in the parking lot so she'll think she's back in the mountains.

Your mama makes that cheese wad casserole again. Now somebody's got to give Grandpa a dishwater enema.

Uncle Muck nails a big ol' Are-O-See Cola sign to the barn to keep it from falling down.

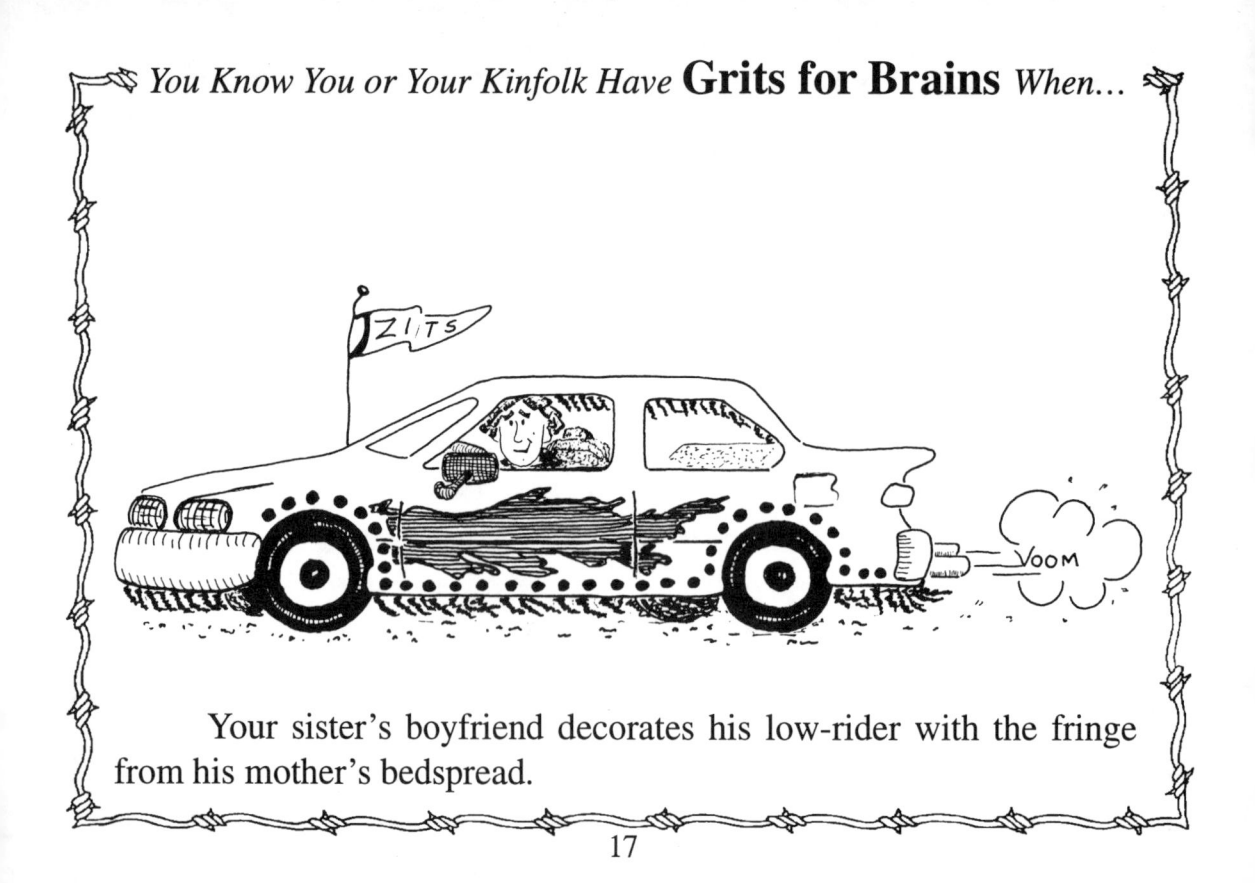

You Know You or Your Kinfolk Have **Grits for Brains** *When...*

Your sister's boyfriend decorates his low-rider with the fringe from his mother's bedspread.

You Know You or Your Kinfolk Have **Grits for Brains** *When...*

Your daddy believes the Alimentary Canal is "somewhere up north."

Your sister, whose talent is waving at cars, is runner-up in the local beauty contest. Unfortunately, Sister is no match for the winner, who not only can stick out her tongue and lick her eyebrows, but has a replica of the American flag trimmed into the hair on her back.

Your daddy can pass wind all the way from the front porch to the pigsty before his pucker strain gives out.

You Know You or Your Kinfolk Have **Grits for Brains** *When...*

Your chameleon takes one look at Cousin Claudie's plaid prom dress with the florescent ruffles and explodes.

You Know You or Your Kinfolk Have **Grits for Brains** *When...*

The county extension agent has to keep reminding your mama that highway meat is not one of the major food groups.

You Know You or Your Kinfolk Have **Grits for Brains** *When...*

At least three of your cousins claim they've been abducted by space aliens.

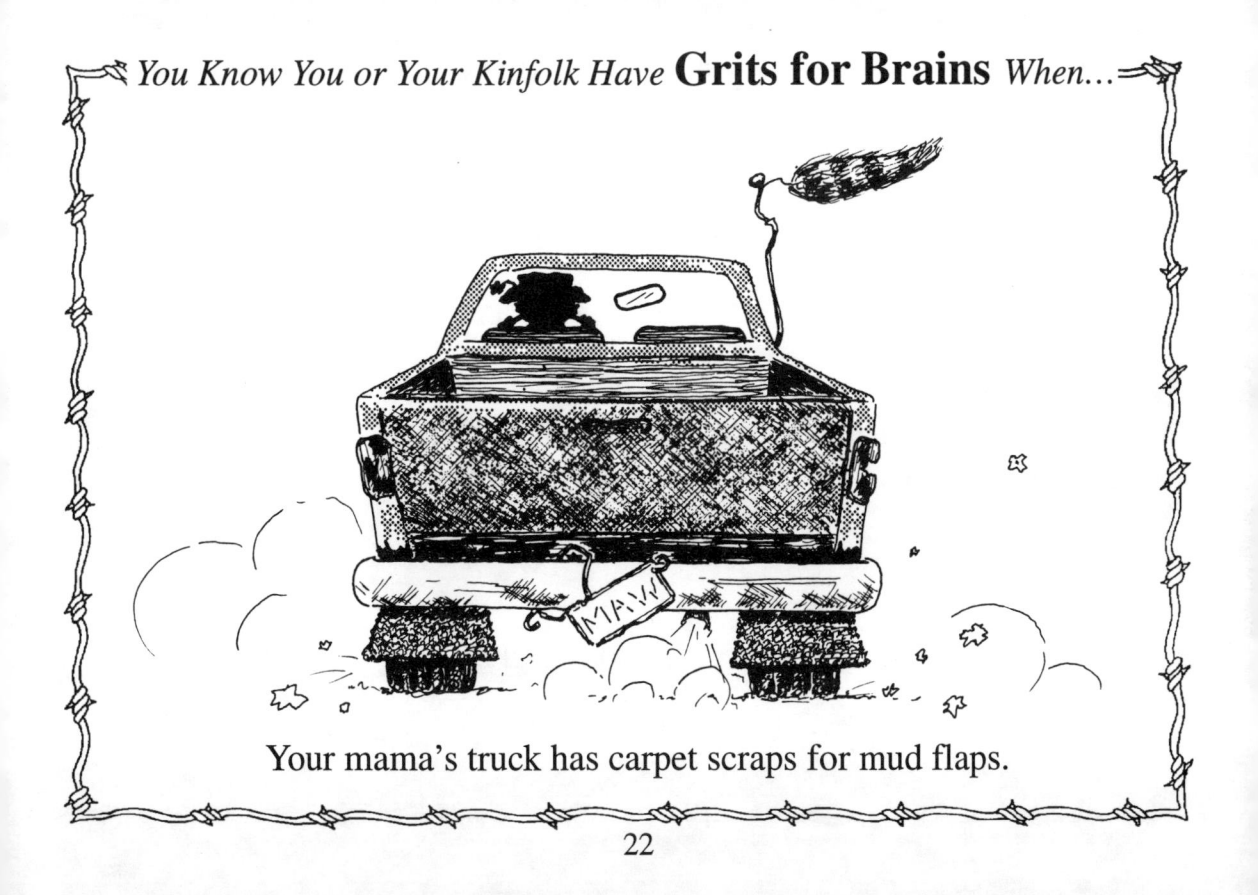

You Know You or Your Kinfolk Have **Grits for Brains** *When...*

Your mama's truck has carpet scraps for mud flaps.

You Know You or Your Kinfolk Have **Grits for Brains** *When...*

Your clan thinks people who collect dryer lint are showing off because they own an electrical appliance.

At the dinner table, your sister tells her kids to clean their plates and they remove their false teeth and start licking them.

Some of the ingredients in your trail mix are moving.

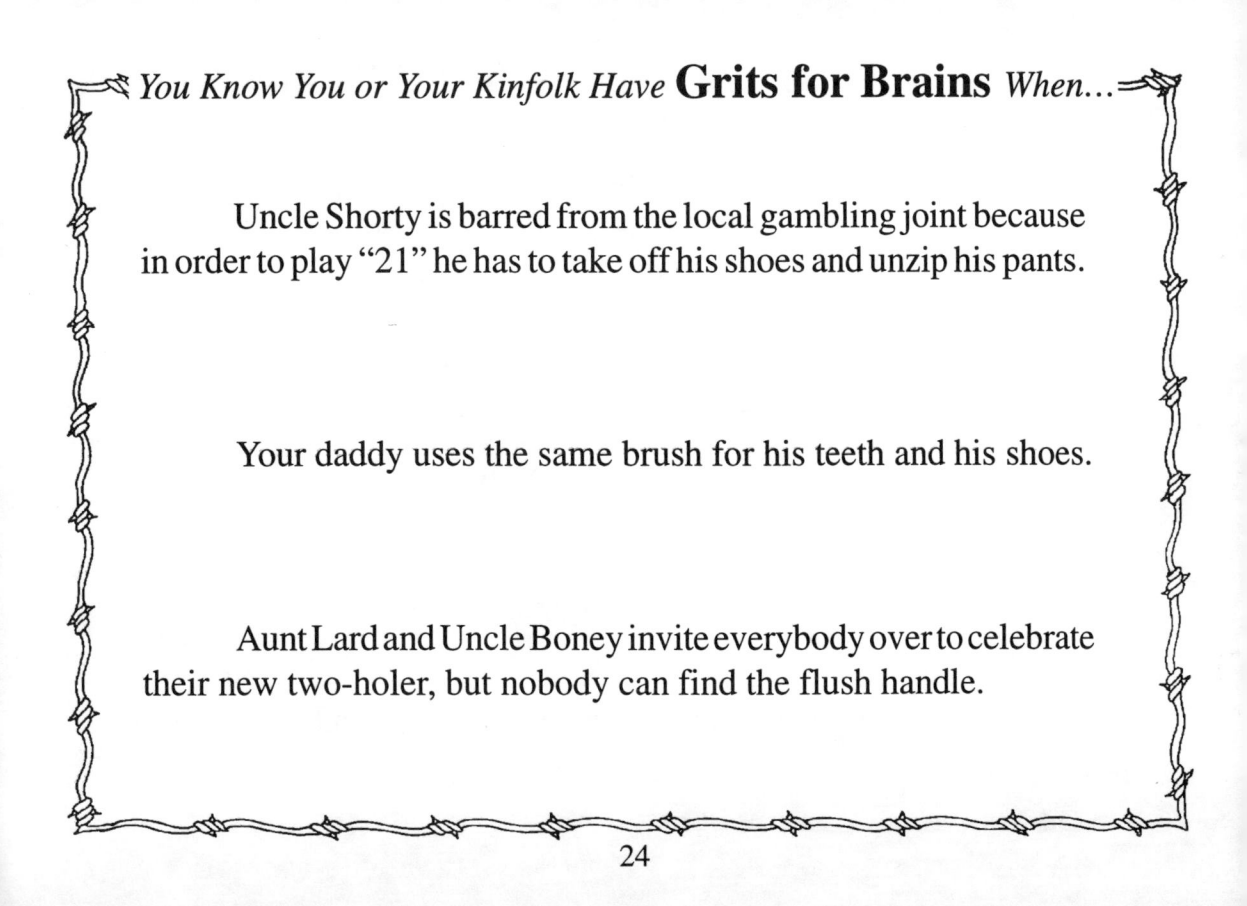

You Know You or Your Kinfolk Have **Grits for Brains** *When...*

Uncle Shorty is barred from the local gambling joint because in order to play "21" he has to take off his shoes and unzip his pants.

Your daddy uses the same brush for his teeth and his shoes.

Aunt Lard and Uncle Boney invite everybody over to celebrate their new two-holer, but nobody can find the flush handle.

You Know You or Your Kinfolk Have **Grits for Brains** *When...*

Your mama's cowgirl hat is wider than her hips and contains more plumage than a feather duster.

You Know You or Your Kinfolk Have **Grits for Brains** *When...*

Your family votes to ban Shakespeare's *King Lear* from the school library because it sounds pornographic.

You Know You or Your Kinfolk Have **Grits for Brains** *When...*

You read the cereal box without moving your lips and your cousins think you are showing off.

The doctor mentions something about purging your mama's colon and she thinks he's criticizing her punctuation.

Your mama's idea of a gourmet meal is a main course with no tire marks.

You Know You or Your Kinfolk Have **Grits for Brains** *When...*

Aunt Flay has her living room painted the same shade of blue as that bad vein in her leg.

You Know You or Your Kinfolk Have **Grits for Brains** *When...*

Granny slings the head off whatever is walking around the yard on Saturday and it's on the table come dinner time Sunday.

You Know You or Your Kinfolk Have **Grits for Brains** *When...*

Your cousin, "Stick-'em-up Stella," who's getting married on the back porch come Thursday, paints that ankle bracelet the law gave her a fine shade of way-off-white so it'll match her wedding overalls.

Your mama isn't worried about mice because the dust balls under her bed look like cats.

Your bath soap is so fuzzy the kids won't put it in the tub for fear of drowning it.

You Know You or Your Kinfolk Have **Grits for Brains** *When...*

Your daughter doesn't understand why she can't fly if she wears a winged feminine pad.

You Know You or Your Kinfolk Have **Grits for Brains** *When...*

You splash on your new cologne and somebody asks, "Who stepped in cow flop?"

You find yourself trying to talk Aunt Humpel out of having her trick pelvis "healed" by the Reverend Mooney Slide, who wants to lay hands on it.

Company is coming and Cousin Fade, the artist, floats a butter sculpture of Junior Samples in the vegetable soup.

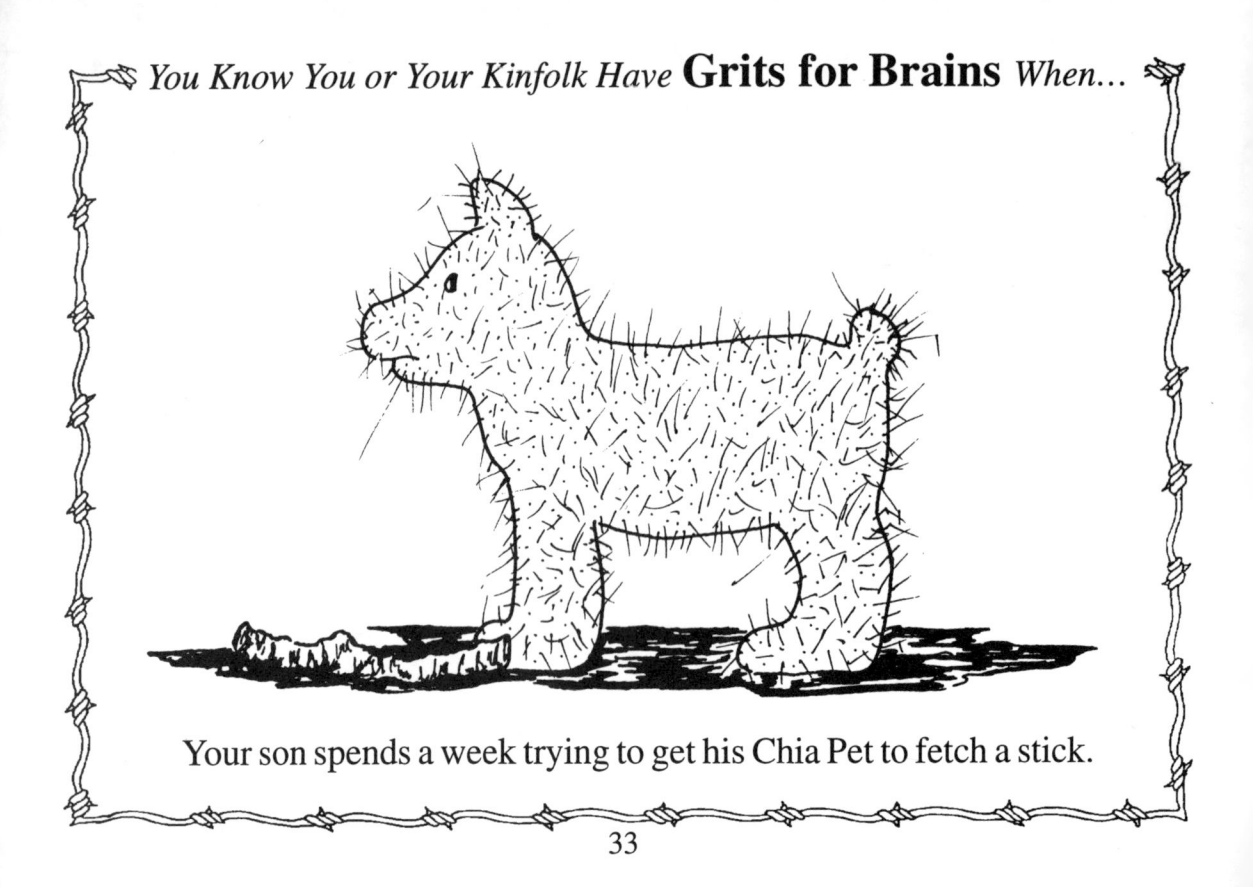

You Know You or Your Kinfolk Have **Grits for Brains** *When...*

Your son spends a week trying to get his Chia Pet to fetch a stick.

You Know You or Your Kinfolk Have **Grits for Brains** *When...*

Your sister swallows a mouthful of dimes because she doesn't own a purse and she can't find her pocket.

You Know You or Your Kinfolk Have **Grits for Brains** *When...*

Cousin Sweeney cold-cocks a reporter because she asks if he plans to become bi-coastal after winning the lottery and a house in California.

Your son thinks the governor's middle finger is the state bird.

Nobody in the family understands why it's been so difficult finding a good second-hand casket for Uncle Newton.

You Know You or Your Kinfolk Have **Grits for Brains** *When...*

Your cat catches ringworm from your sister.

You Know You or Your Kinfolk Have **Grits for Brains** *When...*

Aunt Thurl calls to say she is thrilled with her new house back in the mountains but not the washing machine that came with it. Seems she put five shirts in it, pulled the chain, and they disappeared.

You were 14 before you realized that cottage cheese is not supposed to be green and crunchy.

Your mama decides not to shave her mustache after winning the Merle Haggard look alike contest.

You Know You or Your Kinfolk Have **Grits for Brains** *When...*

Somebody yells "Let's go bitch," at your family reunion and every woman within earshot heads for her husband's pickup truck.

Your clan's coat of arms shows a 'possum impaled on a dinner fork.

Your male relatives admit that a woman who can siphon gas through a length of tire hose is more desirable than a long-bed truck loaded with bird dogs.

You Know You or Your Kinfolk Have **Grits for Brains** *When…*

Your mama's leg hairs are longer than the dog's.

You Know You or Your Kinfolk Have **Grits for Brains** *When...*

The weather gets hot and everybody has to take turns fanning the flies off Grandpa.

Your sister names her baby Graceland and swears she once spotted Elvis at a Barbecue joint ordering a hog to go.

Granny closes the bathroom door and whatever's going on sounds like a ball pean hammer hitting a cow bell. Now you'll have to bondo the inside of the porcelain convenience, because she's getting way too much iron in her diet.

You Know You or Your Kinfolk Have **Grits for Brains** *When...*

Everybody you know keeps a can of fishing worms in the refrigerator.

You Know You or Your Kinfolk Have **Grits for Brains** *When...*

You've named Mama's muskrat fur "Clyde" because, due to age and oxidation, it's now the same shade of orange as the orangutan in that Clint Eastwood movie.

You Know You or Your Kinfolk Have **Grits for Brains** *When...*

Your daddy switches from boxer to jockey-type shorts because he says boxers make him feel like a grandfather clock — the pendulum is always swinging and it's always 6:30.

Uncle Buster nearly hangs himself when he gets his foot caught in his suspenders while squatting on General Sherman's statue.
Buster gave liquor as an excuse. The police gave Buster 30 days and the widow Banger gave up astronomy after witnessing this particular eclipse of the moon.

You Know You or Your Kinfolk Have **Grits for Brains** *When...*

There are more pictures of your family on the walls of the U.S. Post Office than in the family photo album.

You Know You or Your Kinfolk Have **Grits for Brains** *When...*

Your daddy tries to make a window fan out of an airplane propeller and the last time you saw the side of the house it was headed toward I-85.

You Know You or Your Kinfolk Have **Grits for Brains** *When...*

Your mama won't let you date the circus clown because she's afraid he'll try to have carnival knowledge of you.

You Know You or Your Kinfolk Have **Grits for Brains** *When...*

Your daddy asks you what has four wheels, three teeth, is hot and cold and eats doughnuts, and it turns out to be a carload of your mama's menopausal sisters who've just raided the Bonzai Bakery and now can't regulate the thermostat.

It's Thanksgiving and the bird is in the oven, but you can't get the turkey baster until Grandpa is finished with his nose drops and cousin Beumadene does that insemination thing.

You Know You or Your Kinfolk Have **Grits for Brains** *When...*

Your brother wears his earphone radio to Aunt Lornette's funeral because it is held the same day as the Daytona 500.

You Know You or Your Kinfolk Have **Grits for Brains** *When...*

Your daddy does his own hair transplant from his armpits, using tweezers to pluck and a dinner fork to plant.

You Know You or Your Kinfolk Have **Grits for Brains** *When...*

Aunt Lilt fills in furniture scratches with ear wax.

Your grandpa and grandma nickname each other's crotchal regions. Granny calls his "Mr. Johnson," after the old fella down the road who dribbles a lot and can't get up and about much anymore. He calls hers "Eleanor Roosevelt," because, according to Grandpa, "It ain't the best looking thing in the world, but it gets the job done."

You Know You or Your Kinfolk Have **Grits for Brains** *When...*

Your mama buys Brother a truss because the English teacher says his dangling participles are causing him problems.

You Know You or Your Kinfolk Have **Grits for Brains** *When...*

You photocopy your naked backside down at the plant on April Fool's Day, put a copy of it on the bulletin board, and Cousin Sumpter asks if that feller is kin to you because he notices a family resemblance somewhere around the eye.

Every time you take your mama to the free clinic you have to remind her that the liquid in the little jars is not complimentary juice.

Your mama says her stretch marks and varicose veins combined approximate a map of the state highway system.

You Know You or Your Kinfolk Have **Grits for Brains** *When...*

    Your sister has a baby, but you won't know if you're an aunt or uncle until somebody tells you if it was a boy or a girl.

    Somebody tells Uncle Loomis that crotch crickets make good bait and now he goes fishing with only a pole and a comb.

    Your kids see a "Watch for Falling Rock" sign in the mountains and think a Native American celebrity is in town.

You Know You or Your Kinfolk Have **Grits for Brains** *When...*

The men in the family fasten their safety belts around their six-packs and put their wives in the back seat.

Your mama dislocates her hip in the ladies room down at the beer joint after they run out of toilet tissue and she tries to dry something other than her hands with the hot air machine.

The dental hygienist doesn't return your calls because the last time you got your teeth cleaned bell-bottoms were in style and you'd just eaten an onion/peanut sandwich and a handful of chocolate cookies.

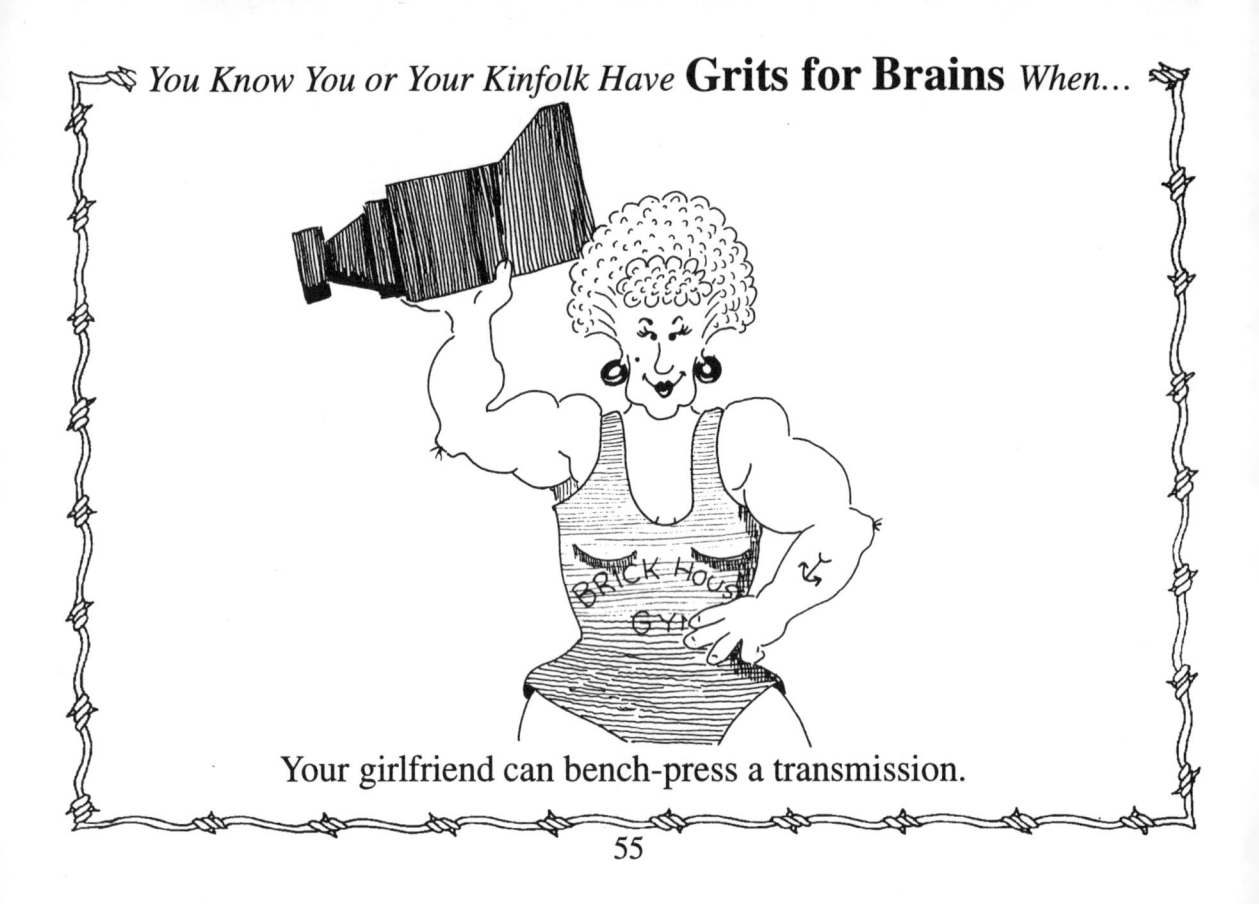

You Know You or Your Kinfolk Have **Grits for Brains** *When...*

Your girlfriend can bench-press a transmission.

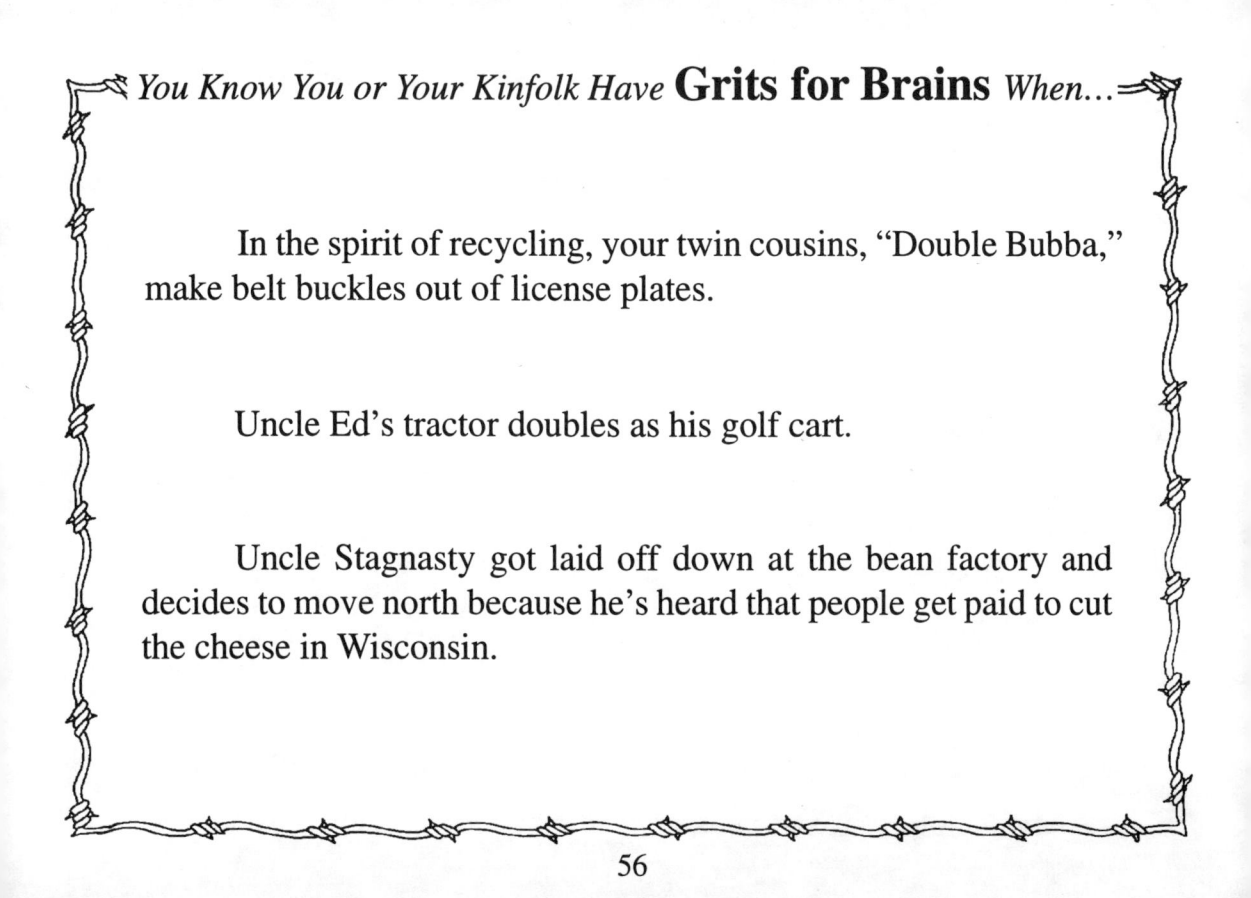

You Know You or Your Kinfolk Have **Grits for Brains** *When...*

In the spirit of recycling, your twin cousins, "Double Bubba," make belt buckles out of license plates.

Uncle Ed's tractor doubles as his golf cart.

Uncle Stagnasty got laid off down at the bean factory and decides to move north because he's heard that people get paid to cut the cheese in Wisconsin.

You Know You or Your Kinfolk Have **Grits for Brains** *When…*

Grandpa uses Granny's bloomers to seine for mullet.

You Know You or Your Kinfolk Have **Grits for Brains** *When...*

Your husband believes that: professional wrestling is on the level; he has a chance to make big money from the poker machine down at the service station; white socks go with everything; and Burt Reynolds' hair is real.

Your mama hunkers naked over a hand-mirror to put salve on a carbuncle and can't figure out who that is smiling back at her.

Your wife thinks a "cow pie" has something to do with pastry.

You Know You or Your Kinfolk Have **Grits for Brains** *When...*

Your sister discovers her new boyfriend's nickname, "Bill," is short for "Billboard" the day she sees his special tattoo grow from "Eat at Joe's" to "Eat at Joe's — Finest Food in The State, Ample Seating, No Waiting, Visa And Master Card Accepted."

You Know You or Your Kinfolk Have **Grits for Brains** *When...*

Your truck breaks down, Uncle Boney lets you borrow his station wagon and everybody fights over who gets to ride up on the luggage rack.

Granny takes to perching on the satellite dish to receive secret messages from a TV evangelist.

Grandpa sends the tent preacher a get-well card because next Sunday's sermon deals with being caught up in the rapture and he thinks the Reverend might have gotten his privates tangled in barbed wire.

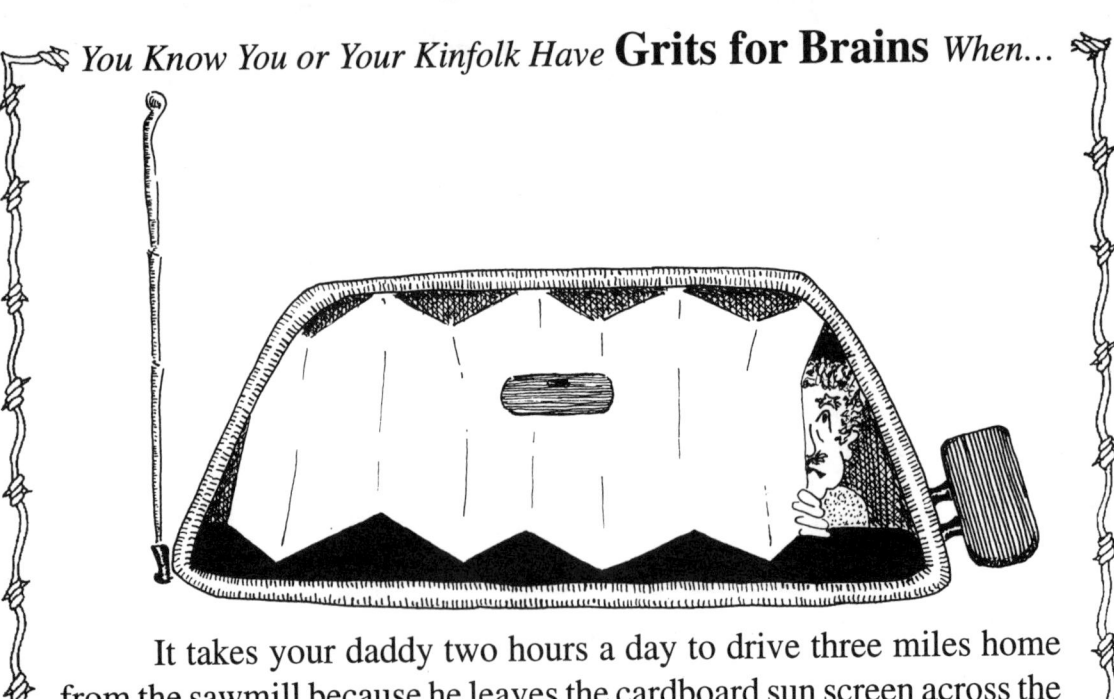

You Know You or Your Kinfolk Have **Grits for Brains** *When...*

It takes your daddy two hours a day to drive three miles home from the sawmill because he leaves the cardboard sun screen across the windshield.

You Know You or Your Kinfolk Have **Grits for Brains** *When...*

It's 110 in the shade, Junior is packin' a load and when you change his diaper, it sets off the smoke alarm.

Your sister has nicotine stains on more than her fingers since she started saving filter tips from cigarettes to use as tampons.

Aunt Marlene sprays so much spice air freshener in her house that you don't know if Uncle Homer's socks have started to fester or if she's just baked another bad fruit cake.

You Know You or Your Kinfolk Have **Grits for Brains** *When...*

The trees in your mama's front yard are whitewashed halfway up so they'll match the tractor tire flower pot and Mexican donkey cart.

Your kids save the family scabs and use them for checkers.

Your sister takes half a cup of ammonia and adds it to a bucket of the dog's bath water to remove her footprints from the ceiling of the pickup truck after a Saturday night date.

You Know You or Your Kinfolk Have **Grits for Brains** *When...*

Your mama starts making lampshades from fast food chicken buckets and your wife thinks they'll make mighty fine Christmas gifts.

You Know You or Your Kinfolk Have **Grits for Brains** *When...*

Your brother-in-law has saved enough broken bed slats to build a rustic fence.

Grandpa accuses the neighbors of getting uppity since they put a tennis ball on their trailer hitch.

Cousin Luther runs out of cat-head biscuits and uses the car sponge to sop the rest of his red-eye gravy.

You Know You or Your Kinfolk Have **Grits for Brains** *When...*

Your brother thinks the rhythm method of birth control has to do with the song that's playing on the radio during foreplay.

Your sister provides pan-flute music for the neighbors' outdoor wedding by flying through the air on a tire swing with rollers in her hair.

Your mama is arrested down at the A&P after she spies the ribbed condoms in her grocery cart and the chicken she heaves at you hits a customer by mistake.

You Know You or Your Kinfolk Have **Grits for Brains** *When...*

Your son thinks those little O's in his cereal bowl are donut seeds.

You Know You or Your Kinfolk Have **Grits for Brains** *When...*

Your sister decides not to hide her talent under a bushel and shows the preacher how to make an armpit toot during Sunday dinner and now there are cat faces in the tablecloth where Granny gripped it.

Your sister can make her navel smoke a cigarette.

Your brother tells you he learned that the Lord's middle initial was "H" the night Grandpa hit his thumb with the hammer while hanging the Christmas stockings.

You Know You or Your Kinfolk Have **Grits for Brains** *When...*

Your wife furnishes three rooms of the trailer by "shopping" in town at the curbside on trash pick-up day.

You tell Cousin Archie you lost a hub cap and he tries to lend you his hat.

Your mama talks the congregation out of buying a chandelier for the church because, "Nobody would know how to play it."

You Know You or Your Kinfolk Have **Grits for Brains** *When...*

Uncle Feemster gets drunk down at the D.C. railroad yard, mistakes the tracks for steps and the rails for bannisters and crawls three miles before he realizes he isn't in the Washington Monument.

You discover that Great-uncle Corley, the one who drowned in a barrel of whiskey mash, got out and went to the bathroom three times before drawing his last breath.

Uncle Dorse tries to make a sailboat out of a door, a rake and a bedsheet.

You Know You or Your Kinfolk Have **Grits for Brains** *When...*

Uncle Jeeter tries to hatch a coconut because he thinks it's a mule egg.

You Know You or Your Kinfolk Have **Grits for Brains** *When...*

Granny's furry robe has no lapels and only one sleeve because they've outlawed shooting rats down at the dump.

You Know You or Your Kinfolk Have **Grits for Brains** *When...*

Your brother-in-law, the carpenter, decides to go into show business and takes "Slate Foyer" as his stage name.

You Know You or Your Kinfolk Have **Grits for Brains** *When...*

Your 30-year-old brother, who is training to become a Flying Elvi, pins a towel to his shirt and jumps off the barn.

You Know You or Your Kinfolk Have **Grits for Brains** *When...*

Your mama finds herself writing very slowly while corresponding with her brother because she knows he can't read fast.

Your mama seats the relatives with the worst drools near the potted plants at family gatherings.

Your brother spends 30 minutes in a revolving door because he can't remember if he's going in, coming out or experiencing *de ja vu.*

You Know You or Your Kinfolk Have **Grits for Brains** *When...*

Your daddy sometimes sits on the bed naked, except for one sock, until he can remember whether he's getting dressed or undressed.

You Know You or Your Kinfolk Have **Grits for Brains** *When...*

Your baldheaded grandpa thinks hair tonic is a health drink.

You Know You or Your Kinfolk Have **Grits for Brains** *When...*

Uncle Grudney "Dog Chow" Griggs hasn't bathed in so long that every time he sweats, he makes his own gravy.

You Know You or Your Kinfolk Have **Grits for Brains** *When...*

You have to tell your husband that passing gas in the new hot tub will not give friends the impression that he bought the model with the extra-jumbo water jet.

Your son, the real pale one, writes a mayonnaise company and asks if he can be their poster boy.

Your visiting mother-in-law believes you are "of the devil," because the short hairs she found between the sheets form a perfect "6 6 6."

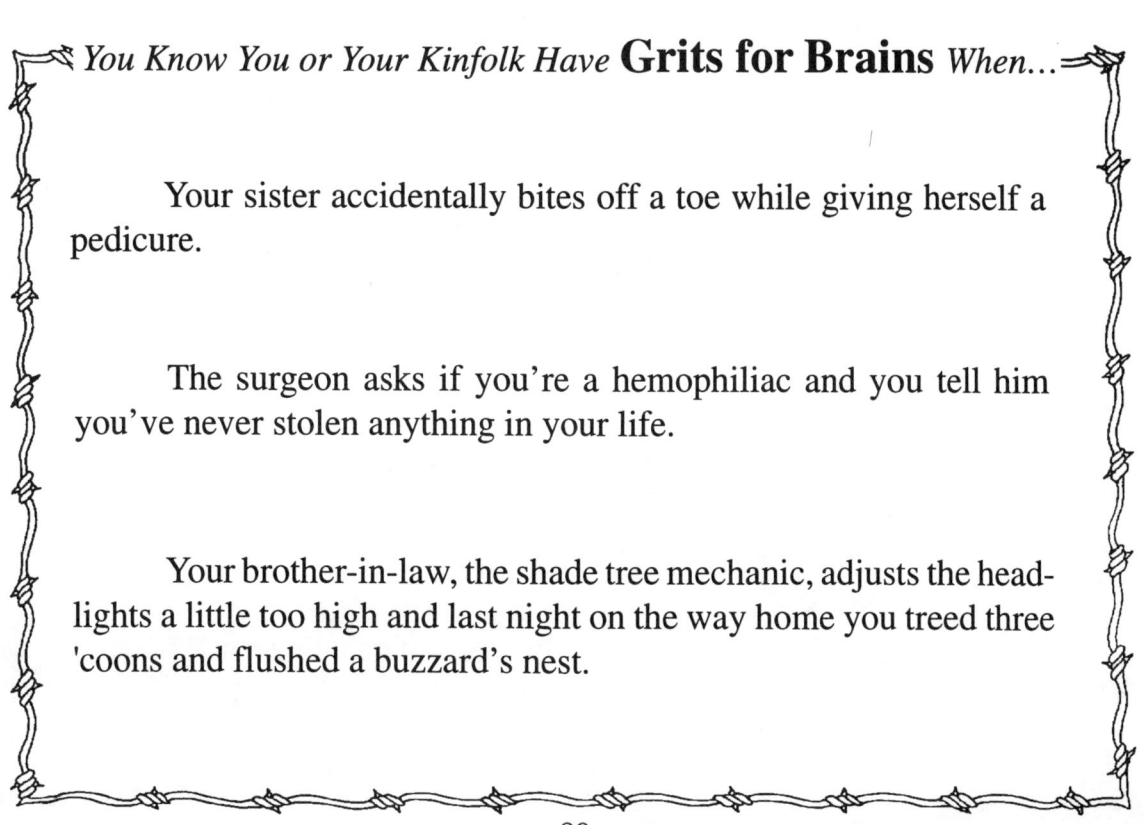

You Know You or Your Kinfolk Have **Grits for Brains** *When...*

Your sister accidentally bites off a toe while giving herself a pedicure.

The surgeon asks if you're a hemophiliac and you tell him you've never stolen anything in your life.

Your brother-in-law, the shade tree mechanic, adjusts the headlights a little too high and last night on the way home you treed three 'coons and flushed a buzzard's nest.

You Know You or Your Kinfolk Have **Grits for Brains** *When...*

Fat Uncle Grover jogs past a container of gasoline while wearing corduroy pants and the resulting explosion blows the roof off the tool shed.

You Know You or Your Kinfolk Have **Grits for Brains** *When...*

Your brother, the gynecologist, puts his patients up on cement blocks instead of in stirrups.

Your confused cousin Cletus thinks the Big Dipper sang "Chantilly Lace" and Roy Orbison Had something to do with the planets moving around the sun.

The last time your girlfriend went barefooted, you complimented her on her alligator shoes.

You Know You or Your Kinfolk Have **Grits for Brains** *When…*

There are more empty beer cans in the long-bed of your pickup than in the dumpster down at the gas station.

You Know You or Your Kinfolk Have **Grits for Brains** *When...*

You decorate your Christmas tree with a tow rope, paper cups and potted meat pull-tabs.

You Know You or Your Kinfolk Have **Grits for Brains** *When...*

It's February 2nd and your sister is pouting because everybody is paying attention to the groundhog instead of her and she can cast a whole lot bigger shadow.

You Know You or Your Kinfolk Have **Grits for Brains** *When...*

Cousin Brack complains that he'll never know who his great-grandma was because somebody took a chainsaw to the family tree out back.

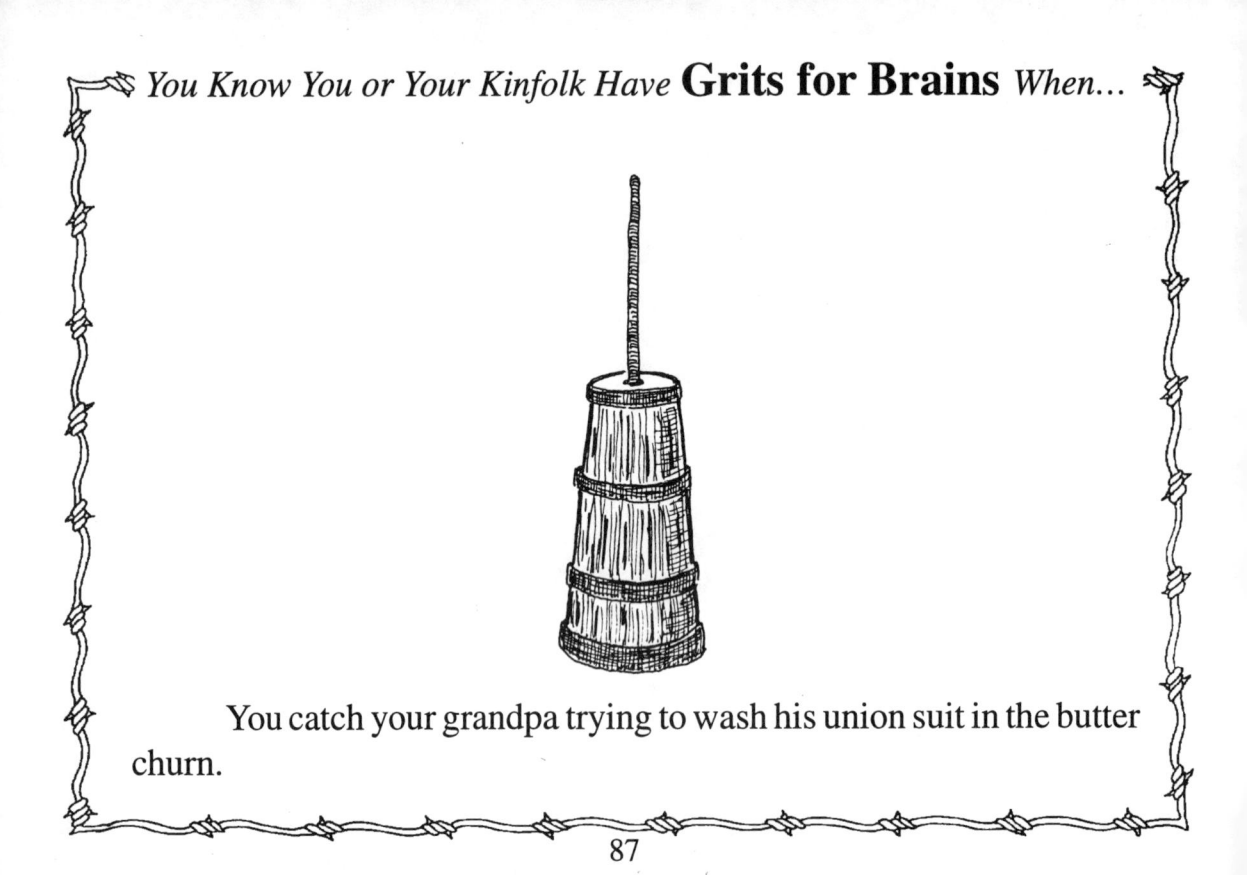

You Know You or Your Kinfolk Have **Grits for Brains** *When...*

You catch your grandpa trying to wash his union suit in the butter churn.

You Know You or Your Kinfolk Have **Grits for Brains** *When...*

You name your son "Neon" in hopes that he'll be bright enough to graduate grammar school by age 18.

You Know You or Your Kinfolk Have **Grits for Brains** *When...*

Your cousin Scant, the family tycoon, clips the remote control to his belt so folks will think he's wearing a beeper.

Your sister thinks a *bidet* is a painting by a French Impressionist.

Your son's history teacher keeps reminding him it's Plato and Pliny, not Pluto and Minnie.

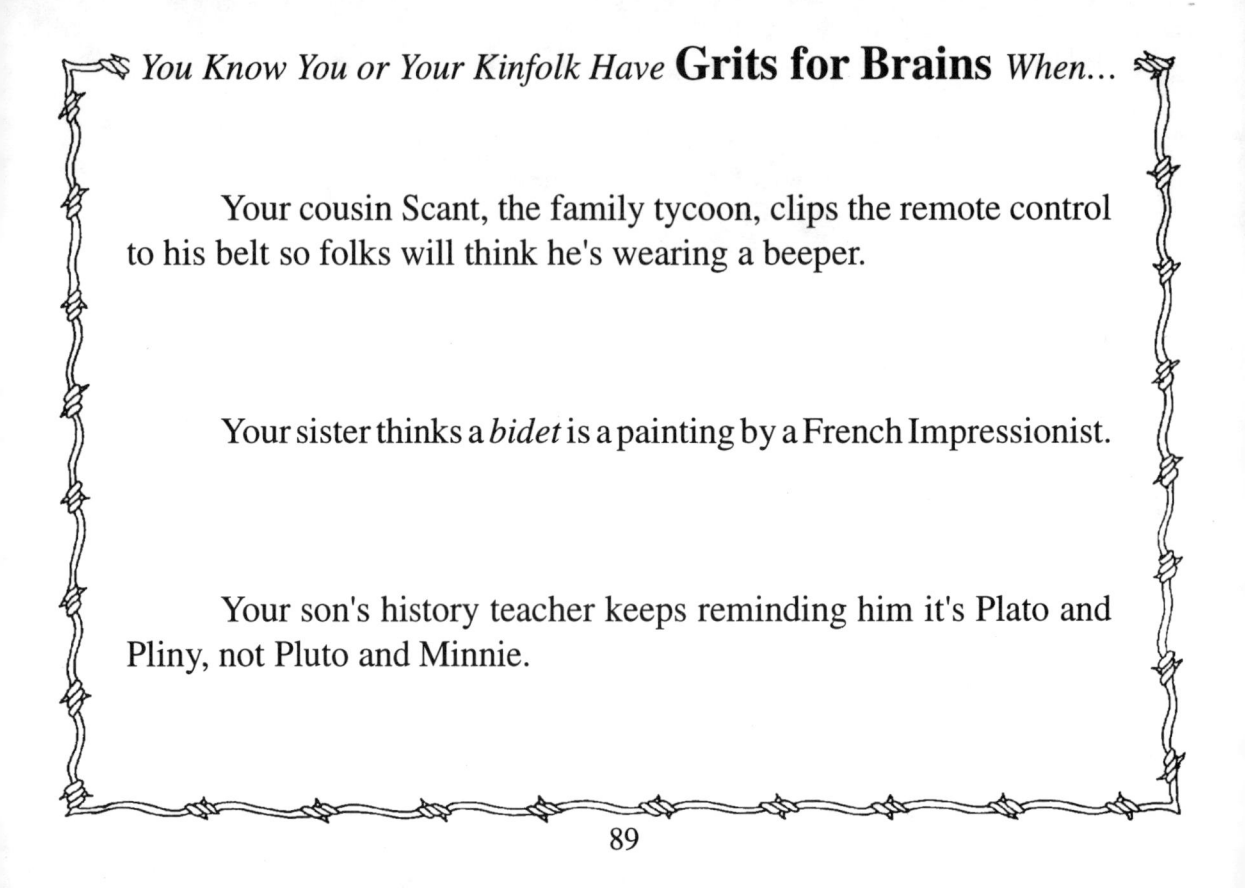